Tender Loving Care for Pet Birds

T. J. LAFEBER, D.V.M.

Dorothy Products
818 S. Seminary
Park Ridge, Ill. 60068

Through all of our lives, birds abound about us in their bright, cheerful manner. When taken into our homes, it is our desire to have them continue their happy ways. The goal of this booklet is to help you keep your bird healthy, happy, and alive to an old age.

TABLE OF CONTENTS

1 VALUE OF BIRDS

Birds are the Most Underrated Pet.

The value of pet birds to their owners can only be appreciated by personal experience. In many instances, birds are the most ideal pet that a person could have.

Birds Contribute Personal Value to the Owner.

Companionship - Having pet owner love and feel loved may be the greatest contribution made by pets. Birds are companion animals.

Overcoming loneliness
Entertainment and enjoyment
Beauty
Recreation, hobby
Pride of ownership
Brings nature into our lives

Birds are Probably the Greatest Wonder of the World.

In all creation there is nothing more unusual and beautiful than birds.

Birds are One of the Least Understood of Our Pets.

There is no animal that is seen more and yet is more mysterious.

Birds are One of the Hardiest of World's Creatures.

Their endurance is noted through evolutionary survival and as documented by their hardiness and resistance to medical problems.

From the Dawn of Civilization, Birds Have Been Deeply Involved in Our Lives.

Birds are the Most Undervalued Pet.

Though the actual purchase price may be expensive, for some inexplicable reason, birds have always been underpriced.

Is it Fair to Make a Pet Out of a Bird?

Life in the wild is hazardous for birds. Probably those who die a natural death are in the minority.

The life of a bird in a home is one of longevity if the owner assumes the proper responsibility.

2

Bird Care is Relatively Easy.

Because of their size and basic requirements, the average person will not be burdened with even the ultimate in bird care.

A Bird Can be an Asset to Any Home.

Nothing will add to a room quite like a bird: plants, tropical fish, rocks are fine, but a bird is the best.

Birds Can Contribute Both Within the Home and Within the Greater Community.

Concerned parents may use birds as an acceptable method of motivating their children and teaching responsibility.

Teachers use pet birds in classroom situations to add excitement and interest.

Pet birds have an advantage when used in rehabilitation programs for people who are physically handicapped, mentally disturbed, retarded, hospitalized or confined to nursing homes or correctional facilities.

2 NUTRITION OF PET BIRDS

Improper feeding is the chief cause of disease and death in pet birds. A balanced diet is the single most important responsibility that the pet owner has.

Pet birds suffer from nutritional problems partially from their high metabolic rate. The chemical reactions that are continuously taking place inside the bird are going on at a much more rapid rate than in mammals. The speed of this activity requires an unusual amount of fuel. Because the bird is burning this fuel (protein, carbohydrates, fats, vitamins and minerals) at a much higher rate than mammals, shortage will be noticed more quickly. A lack of essential nutrients could be noticed in the bird in less than half the time that it would take in a mammal.

Living in a caged environment with food constantly available causes the bird to become very selective in his eating, and he generally restricts his diet to one or two types of seeds. These birds are "picky eaters." The only thing that can result from this type of "picky eating" is gradual malnutrition. Malnourished birds are less active, don't sing, don't talk, have shorter lives, are expensive, may lose weight, have improper molts, and are susceptible to any type of infection.

Nutritional deficiencies are manifest in a number of different ways and not necessarily as having a skinny body. Even a fat bird may have serious nutritional problems. Everything possible must be done to promote good eating habits and good nutrition.

Proper Eating Habits—Twice a Day Feeding

Good eating habits promote a healthier bird. A healthy bird is happy and moves about in a bright, cheerful manner.

When a bird is eating from hunger instead of desire, he may accept a variety of foods. People who come to the dinner table without having snacks in the afternoon are very receptive to the meal placed before them. Birds intuitively feel the same.

Are you killing your bird with kindness by leaving food in the dish continuously?

Pet birds, if in the wild, would mainly feed twice daily. It is unnatural and abnormal for these birds to have food in front of them continuously. Better to take example from nature and feed twice daily.

Twice a day feeding has been proven to be the normal and correct

Feed Your Bird at Mealtime

method of feeding a pet bird. This deviation from tradition may seem startling, but the concept is sound.

Food should be placed in the bird's eating area for a period of time in the morning and in the evening, and then removed. For some birds, ten minutes will be sufficient. Others will require 30–45 minutes. Fresh water should always be in the cage. Greens, along with a piece of fruit or vegetable, may be left in the cage all day.

The average owner has never really watched his bird eat. He must be educated to observe exactly what part of the seed mixture is being consumed. This is particularly important if the bird becomes sick. A malnutrition problem underlying a respiratory infection or diarrhea will not respond to antibiotics or therapy. Sometimes, the only way a deficiency will be suspected will be from the sharp observations of the owner recognizing a selective eater.

ADVANTAGES

Pet birds quickly relate to the person or persons doing the feeding and become their friends. The anticipation of the owner coming to feed stimulates the bird and increases the thrill of being fed.

Feeding time becomes a special time as the bird desires the food, the social activity, and the attention of the owner. He may eat from a hand-held dish and eventually from the hand. Soon the owner will be able to rub his head and stroke his neck, and as the bird feels more secure, he may perch on your finger, shoulder, arm or head.

Overeating has less chance of becoming a problem with this method of feeding.

CHANGES IN EATING HABITS

Sick birds may be recognized by a decreased appetite. The bird owner who is feeding twice a day has a method of measuring daily the bird's intake and will quickly notice any decrease in the amount of food eaten. This is the time to talk to the veterinarian—at the first sign of any abnormality.

Other problems which may be recognized by the owner are these:

Overeating of grit
Not eating the cuttle bone, oyster shells, mineral block, or drinking milk
Difficulty hulling seed
Difficulty eating
Problems swallowing
Vomiting

A regurgitating bird shakes his head to clean his mouth causing mucous and vomitus to cover his feathers.

DIET

Balanced diets are achieved by having your bird eat a variety of foods. To have a completely balanced diet, it must contain 34 separate ingredients. It would be naive to believe that one or two seeds could achieve this goal. Only a bird eating a diversity of foodstuffs will obtain proper nutrition.

What's the best food for my bird?

SEEDS

Consider having two or three cups of seed and seed mixtures available to the bird. These should contain:

Basic seed mix
Supplemental seed
Fresh seeds

The basic diet for most pet birds is a variety of seeds. Some mixtures of seed have been accepted as being the most essential and are packaged commercially as Finch, Canary, Parakeet and Parrot seed.

It is very difficult for the average person to know if he is purchasing a quality bird seed, and, therefore, he must rely on the integrity and knowledge of either a local breeder or pet shop. Pet birds eating only one type of seed as the large part of its diet are subject to nutritional disturbances; for example, a parrot eating only sunflower seeds or a parakeet eating mostly millet. It is important to avoid products that are chiefly composed of one type of seed. Ideally a mixture should contain more than three or four types of seeds and not more than 65% of any one kind.

It is necessary to support the basic seed mix with supplemental seeds. These have been marketed under such labels as health foods, treats, conditioning food, molting food, song food, etc.

Did you know that fresh seeds are an excellent addition to your bird's diet and can be found in your garden, backyard and in fields? Both grass and plant seeds are good. Some of the more common ones are:

Ryegrass
Timothy
Cockspur
Plantain

Hulls accumulate at the top of the seed dish and form a chaff which may cover the remaining seeds. Birds have been known to die because they would not sort through the collection of hulls to find seeds. When seeds are fed to birds, the hulls must be removed daily.

GREENS

Greens are a valuable addition to your bird's diet. The common table or backyard greens are available and may be used. These vegetables have the reputation of causing diarrhea, which is not true, but they will affect the character of the stool. Greens are bulky foods that pass through the digestive tract rapidly, causing a soft, green stool. Foods high in water add fluid to the body. More urine is produced which adds to the fluidity of the droppings.

Bird at first may overeat greens, but if birds are fed greens consistently, they will eat only a small amount.

Table Greens
Lettuce
Endive
Celery
Carrot tops
Spinach

Backyard Greens
Dandelion
Chickweed
Green branches

RIPE FRUITS AND VEGETABLES

Ripe fruits and vegetables are part of a balanced diet for a bird, but should never be over 25% of the diet.

Fruit
Oranges
Apples
Grapes
Cherries

Vegetables
Carrots (sometimes grated)
Green beans
Peas
Corn on the cob

TABLE FOODS

One method of adding variety and interest to a bird's diet is to include table foods. Since a bird may eat any wholesome food, there should be no hesitancy in trying different ones. Start with introducing small crumbs, so as not to frighten the bird. The disadvantage is that many foods spoil rapidly and must be removed from the feeding dish the same day.

Foods which spoil rapidly:

Cottage cheese
Cooked cereal
Baby foods
Macaroni
Eggs (This is a particularly good food, especially during molting. Generally, eggs should be hard cooked or scrambled.)

More stable foods:

Toast—with butter, peanut butter or jam
Pound cake
Sweet rolls—doughnuts
Cheese
Crackers
Cookies
Dry milk
Corn products (corn flakes, popcorn, corn chips, tacos, ground corn)

Your bird can eat any wholesome food.

PELLETS AND MEALS

Preparations of these types offer a variety of nutrients and are an advantage. Even though they have not been perfected, modern research indicates this may be the food of the future.

LIQUIDS

Considering everything a bird eats, water is the most vital factor in a bird's life. Every cell in the bird's body depends upon water for its existence. A 10% loss of fluid volume causes serious disorders; the loss of 20%, death.

Since most use the same source of water for his birds as for himself, the water supply is generally pure. Self-contamination occurs when droppings fall into the water or seed cups, or when clean water is placed in a dirty container.

Any contaminant or pollutant is potentially dangerous to a bird and may cause death. Birds need pure water, pure food, pure air. Birds are unusually susceptible to most any type of toxin.

In the home, food containers should be washed in the same manner as the family dishes, cleansing water cups every other day and the seed containers once a week. A pet shop or aviary must not only clean but disinfect liquid containers every other day and seed cups once a week.

Other liquids may be offered to pet birds. Some birds have a real fondness for nectars. The Florida and California birds all drink orange juice. Begin sweetening the water with honey, corn syrup, maple syrup, and brown or granulated sugar. After the bird has developed a "sweet tooth" add other nutrients such as juices and milk.

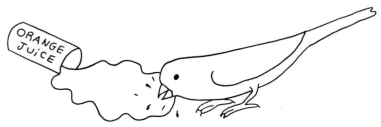

Because birds are by nature suspicious, the addition of a new color in the water or a new food may concern him and he will retreat from the food or water cup. Don't starve your bird. A SMALL BIRD WILL DIE IN 48 HOURS IF IT DOESN'T EAT.

Milk is an excellent food and can be added to the drinking water. Start by adding just enough to color the water. Remember, it must be changed the same day and that any change in color or cloudiness may make him suspicious and he might shun his cup.

GRIT

Grit has long been considered by many aviculturalists as an essential ingredient in the bird's diet. Some question has been raised on this subject. Experience has shown that pet birds that hull their seed digest their food equally well with or without grit.

Seed eating birds seem to have a physiological need for grit in their gizzard. It is natural for them to seek and eat grit. Overeating can irritate and obstruct the gastrointestinal tract. This occurs when the bird is suffering from a deficiency or other ailment.

Grit should be presented in a *grit-mineral* mixture (grit and oyster shells or grit and minerals). Since grit remains in the gizzard for long periods, a few grains daily are sufficient.

VITAMINS

Vitamins should be added to the drinking water. *A specific bird vitamin must be used,* as birds require different amounts and a different Vitamin D than mammals. Specifically, a proportionately larger amount of Vitamin B is required because pet birds hull their seed and thus miss the part of the

13

grain where most of the Vitamin B is stored. The Vitamin D used for mammals is D_2 and birds require D_3.

Bird products containing all these vitamins should be given daily. ALWAYS!!

Vitamin A
vitamin D 3
Vitamin E
Menadione
d-Pantothenic Acid
Niacin

Riboflavin
thiamine Mononitrate
Pyridoxine Hydrochloride
vitamin B 12
Folic Acid
Choline

MINERALS

Minerals are an essential part of the daily diet. The best sources are:

Cuttlebone
Mineral blocks
Milk
Oyster shells
Egg shells

Calcium deficiencies are particularly common in pet birds because they fail to eat the mineral supplements offered to them or their owner doesn't realize the severe shortage of calcium in seeds.

Note for Budgerigar (parakeet) owners:

We have become increasingly aware of the number of thyroid gland disturbances due to a deficiency of iodine in the diet. Because of this, it is now our recommendation that all budgerigars (parakeets) have iodine added to their diet.

The thyroid in an iodine deficient Budgerigar (parakeet) enlarges much the same as a goiter does in a human. This increase in size causes pressure on the windpipe and esophagus. Symptoms of this problem vary considerably from loss of weight and vomiting to mild respiratory noises and difficult breathing.

Birds eating cuttlebone, oyster shells, or balanced mineral block do not require supplemental iodine.

Broadening of Bird's Diet

Many birds have developed poor eating habits, and as a result, have or are bordering on malnutrition. It may be difficult to overcome these bad habits, but persistence usually pays off. Some birds are extremely resistant to having their eating habits changed. Patience and persistence are necessary over a period of weeks, months or years.

You can't starve a pet bird to change his eating habits, but you can nudge him with a little good hunger. Don't starve your bird: remember that a smalll bird will die in 48 hours if it doesn't eat.

Introduce only small amounts of new food or mix new foods with the regular basic seed.

Try hot foods. A bird learns to enjoy hot food as a baby. The body temperature of the mother bird is from 104 to 109, and this is the temperature of the food she feeds her young. Try hot nuts, hot cereals, hot cheese and hot soup.

Place new foods below a mirror or adjacent to a favorite toy.

Try feeding outside of the cage.

Hand or spoon-feed.

Importance of Knowing Your Bird's Daily Food Consumption

A short example may help to emphasize the need to know whether or not a bird is eating and whether or not the volume was adequate. If a loved one ate his breakfast and then was gone for the day and you didn't know whether he ate lunch or not, and then in the evening skipped dinner, the first day you would probably be annoyed. The second time this happened you would probably be irritated and suspicious, but by the time it went on a third or fourth day, it is reasonably certain that you would begin to worry and have the loved one taken to the doctor for an examination and diagnosis.

Problems for your bird may occur which affect appetite and not appearance. The bird may decrease or stop eating and for a while will look perfectly normal. Even the activity can remain vibrant until the bird is near collapse.

At this point, the question should be raised, "How long can a parakeet or small bird go without eating?" A bird will starve to death in 48 hours. To reiterate, the most healthy, even fat finch, canary or parakeet will starve to death in that short period of time because his metabolic rate is so fast that he cannot convert his body tissues into sugars fast enough to supply his energy needs.

Some very sad stories can be told of birds that died of starvation when there was no need for this to happen. Seed cups have filled with hulls and the bird did not know to dig through the hulls to get to seed at the bottom of the cup. Other birds have shied away from their seed cup because of a difference in the shape, color or texture of the food or because something was mixed into the food that frightened him away from it. This can happen with a change of seed or with something new being added to the old food. The suspicious nature of birds, which works for their survival in the wild, can turn against them and cause their demise in captivity. Birds have even died when automatic feeders which were supposed to deliver seed automatically into a cup would become plugged. The transparent vertical container, as would be observed, is full of seed, but the cup below it empty.

The only practical way to evaluate the daily food consumption is to either count droppings or estimate total fecal mass. It would be much more pleasant to measure the food that the bird has eaten out of the cups. Anyone, though, who has tried this becomes completely perplexed by the bird's antics. Sometimes the bird uses its seed as a game and throws it about the cage. They will mix the hulls with the whole seed and to separate these would be a major effort. Birds also use their feed as chew toys and hull their seeds as though to eat them, and then drop both the hull and the germ to the floor of the cage.

Because the bird's digestive system is very short, this causes the food which he eats today to be passed through the intestinal tract the same day. Therefore, the droppings reflect the quantity of food that he has eaten that specific day. A sick bird that is eating only half his regular volume of food will immediately reflect it as a decrease in half the total number of droppings. (In this particular instance the word "dropping" is used to mean fecal material and only the droppings containing feces would be included in the volume.) The white urates and the clear fluid urine would not be included in the total count of the droppings for the day.

Food Dangers

MOLDY FOOD

Unexplained sickness and death in birds may likely be a result of food contaminated with the toxins from fungi. Mold growing on food under favorable environmental conditions can produce harmful compounds. Poisoning occurs when these foods are eaten. Birds may be one of the most susceptible animals to these noxious products.

BUGGY FOOD

To a good housekeeper, the sight of bugs in the seed is very upsetting. They are not harmful to the bird, and actually show there is no pesticide or insecticide in the mix. This buggy seed is not harmful if eaten, and the insects cannot live in the bird nor carry disease. To eliminate the bugs, place the seed on a cookie sheet in a 180° oven for thirty minutes. Never heat the seed over 212°. After thirty minutes, the bugs and their eggs will be dead. These temperatures will not affect the nutritional value of the seed.

DIRTY FOOD

When purchasing seed, check for cleanliness. Grains may be very dusty, have objectionable odors, be contaminated with urine or feces from rodents, or may contain chaff and other foreign fibers. Since this is a food for your pet, you should monitor it closely.

UNWASHED FRUITS AND VEGETABLES

As for yourself, these foods should be washed thoroughly before giving them to your bird. It only takes a small amount of insecticide, herbicide or fungicide to be lethal to your bird.

OVEREATING OF GRIT

In trying to compensate for a nutritional deficiency, a bird is apt to overindulge in grit. This could easily be compared to pouring sand down the kitchen sink. The effects are obvious in the sink. In the bird, it results in either an irritated intestinal tract or a complete obstruction, which would be fatal.

SEED CUPS FILLED WITH HULLS

Cups filled with hulls fool both the owner and the bird—only the bird might die.

EMPTY FOOD AND WATER CONTAINERS

CONTAMINATED WATER AND SEED CONTAINERS

Water and seed containers can become contaminated with dirt or bacteria. Bacterial counts in the water cup can reach enormous proportions in three days. Droppings falling into seed and water cups amplify the problem and are common contaminants.

POISONOUS PLANTS

A number of common houseplants and garden ornamentals are toxic to birds if ingested. Ivy, poinsettia, and a species of dieffenbachia are included in a list of potentially dangerous plants which can be found in CURRENT VETERINARY THERAPY. A bird which has sufficient greens supplied to him in his regular diet will not normally eat poisonous plants.

VITAMIN AND MINERAL DEFICIENCIES

Deficiencies of protein, carbohydrate, fats and minerals develop rapidly. At no time can a person become complacent about the nutrition of his bird.

3 CAGE and FURNISHINGS

After 2,000 years, we are still discovering better ways to house birds. The need for new and innovative designs in bird cages has been precipitated from a newer knowledge that many of our birds are suffering psychological problems brought upon them by their housing.

Once a bird has been removed from his natural environment, then his life in captivity must provide him with the essentials which nature had given. Free flight, first of all, has been used by the bird for food gathering. This food is easily compensated for in captivity. Second, the loss of exercise and freedom does not seem to be a major problem as it adjusts well to limited activity. Third, flight provides a bird with immediate safety, and has been the bird's answer to all types of hostility, suspicion and fear.

The freedom to fly away has, in reality, been the bird's answer to most of his problems and has particularly given him a secure feeling. Therefore, captivity must provide him a substitute for the safety he has lost without flight. This substitute may be a partition that he can hide behind, a hollow log, a nest box, a covered cage, or any area where the bird might feel as though he were hiding. These areas must be accessible to the bird at all times, and, unfortunately, there is no one set shelter that all birds will accept as the perfect security area.

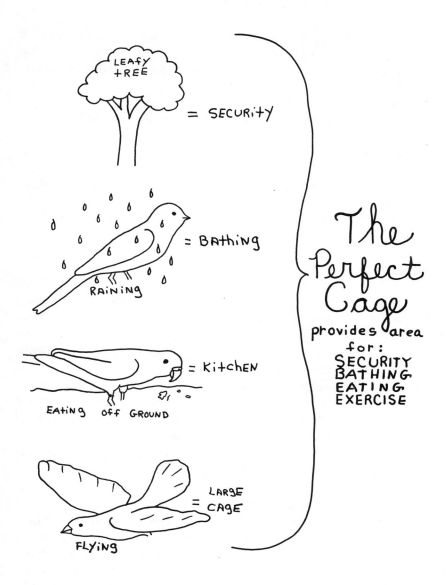

LEAFY
tREE

= SECURITY

RAINING

= BAthing

EAting off GROUND

= Kitchen

FLYing

= LARGE CAGE

The
Perfect
Cage
provides area
for:
SECURITY
BATHING
EATING
EXERCISE

21

A BIRD CAGE SHOULD PROVIDE:

A living area large enough for the bird to extend his wings without touching the sides; perches arranged so his tail will not hit the back of the cage; and sufficient room to jump from one perch to another or to exercise by climbing.

An area for security.

A space where the bird may conveniently be fed twice daily

A bathing area

Seed and water cups located where they will not become contaminated with droppings

Room to place toys or other objects which the bird would use for exercise and entertainment

A tray so that the cage papers are easily removed for daily changing

Cage Paper

Emphasis needs to be placed on the importance of the cage paper and the need to change it daily. Bird droppings have no odor, and without an offensive smell, it is not likely that the pet owner will feel the need to change the cage paper frequently. The proper motivation must come through an understanding and realization of the basic facts.

The first function of the cage paper is to collect the feces and allow you to dispose of them easily and conveniently. Manure building up in the bird's cage—even though it has no appreciable odor—allows bacteria to multiply and results in an unnecessary danger to the bird. As the waste material dries and becomes powdery, currents of air pick up this dust and spread it into the environment contaminating the bird's food and air. Bird droppings are fairly dry within 48 hours. The recommendation, then, is to change the cage paper at 24 hour intervals.

The second reason for changing the cage paper daily is equal in importance to the first. The bird's droppings function as an effective indicator in measuring the bird's health. When the paper is changed frequently, fresh droppings are constantly observed. If the feces are allowed to mound up, interpretation and evaluation is impossible. Details regarding the interpretation of droppings is covered in the section on Digestive System.

To ask the owner of the bird to change the cage paper daily will be unrewarding unless it is easy and convenient to do. Cages are needed which allow the drawer for the paper to be slid out easily without any binding or catching. The paper itself must be cheap and readily accessible. A ready source of an ideal cage paper is newspaper or some other convenient disposable paper. A pattern can be made and eight or ten thicknesses of newspaper cut out. The whole stack of papers is put into the tray. Daily, the top paper is removed. The droppings are examined and counted, and the paper discarded.

Since birds may clip, strip, and chew the cage paper, one concern to those using newspapers is the fear of poisoning from printers ink. Printers ink does contain a small amount of lead. An article published in the American Veterinary Medical Association Journal explained rather conclusively that the lead content is so small that a bird would probably have to consume a whole sheet of newspaper to be in any danger of suffering from lead poisoning.

CHANGE CAGE PAPER DAILY

The psittasine groups of birds, particularly, enjoy clipping and wadding the paper, possibly as part of a nesting habit. Eating the cage paper reflects a depraved appetite and a veterinarian should be consulted.

Often grit is fed to a pet bird by covering the floor of the cage with "gravel paper"—paper cut to fit the bottom of the cage which has grit adhered to it or laying grit loosely on the bottom of the cage. Neither

23

method is an acceptable way of providing grit for the bird. First of all, grit is on the floor where it will be mixed and eaten with the droppings. Secondly, the grit supplied loose or with these papers is not the required grit-mineral mixture.

The other disadvantage to gravel paper is that it must be purchased and a considerable quantity used over the period of one year. The economics are likely to discourage someone from changing the cage paper daily. Newspaper or some other disposable paper will function just as well.

Cage Cover

In the colonial house, birds were in a position of prominence and needed to be protected against the changes in temperatures which occurred as the fires died out during the night. The cage was covered by a heavy cloth or blanket to help retain the heat until morning.

The change in our lifestyle has had both advantages and disadvantages for the bird, and the cage cover is involved. The bird needs the cover today as badly as he did in colonial times, but for entirely different reasons. In our modern living, we have created another problem for birds.

Our sophisticated housing has effectively destroyed some of the environmental influences that helped control the bird's cyclic metabolism.

In the modern home, the temperature, humidity and photoperiods (number of hours of light in the day) are maintained almost stable summer and winter. In effect, there no longer is a change in seasons for the bird to help stimulate and regulate the endocrine (hormone), reproductive and integumentary (skin and feathers, beak and nails) systems.

Another problem created from today's lifestyle involves the number of hours of sleep allowed the bird each night. Because of their susceptibility to light, birds can only sleep when it is dark. Although they will close their eyes during the daylight hours as if sleeping, the presence of the light is still stressing to their system. A room which is light until midnight and re-illuminated at 6:00 A.M., creates only six hours of sleep for the bird. If this is continued night after night, the stress of insufficient sleep will allow physical and neurological problems to develop.

Therefore, cage covers or other methods of controlling the photoperiods are now needed. The bird's cage should be cloaked with a heavy, light tight cover sufficiently well to make it dark. The light should be regulated to correspond to approximately the number of hours of daylight in a day.

Perch

A bird's entire life is spent either standing or flying. The thought of standing most of one's life creates mental pictures of sore, aching feet and legs. A bird not only stands all day long, but also sleeps in the same position with his claws locked around the perch. The only time in his life span, 10–77 years, the bird is off its feet is when the hen is nesting. When not flying, the bird may walk, but generally jumps from place to place, which is a further insult to the already stressed locomotion system.

The material a bird stands on does make a difference. Should the surface be smooth or rough? Should the perch be hard or soft? Should the perch be flexible or rigid? The shape may also be questioned. The answer to these questions will prevent a few of the leg and foot problems that bother our birds.

SHAPES

Although we think of something round when the word "perch" is spoken, there are many shapes. A variety of shapes in the bird's perches is probably more important than a number of round perches of various diameters. The goal must be to have even distribution of weight on the toes and feet in order to prevent pressure sores. Having the toes grip different size and shaped perches conditions all parts of the foot.

Shapes:

Round
Oval
Square
Rectangular

Notice the difference in the pressure points between the types of perches.

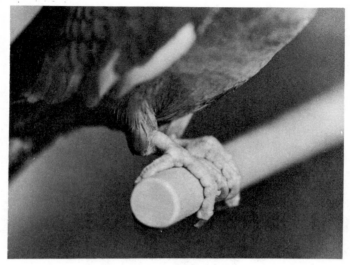

Flat (Birds sometimes prefer to sit with their toes extended on a flat, wide perch. Any board placed across the cage can easily provide for this need)

SOFT PERCHES

With the frequency that foot problems have been encountered in pet birds, it is advisable to have a soft perch in the cage which the bird may use if he desires:

Padded—cotton, cork or carpeting or other soft material

Wrapped—with paper towel, flannel or felt

Soft hose—as suggested under "non-rigid"

RIGID

In observations of aviary birds where both rigid and non-rigid perches were used, the birds about equally divided their time between the two. Both types should be provided for your bird's use.

NON-RIGID

As nature has provided swaying branches, non-rigid perches help to absorb the shock and impact of a bird's landing. As the bird made its adaptation for flight, the bony skeleton became delicate, and therefore a cushioned stop is helpful. A hose stretched across the cage makes an ideal perch, especially if composed of soft rubber or soft plastic.

Swings
String or rope stretched across cage
Perches with a spring end
Branch with small twigs on it

BRANCHES

Nature provides sticks and branches which serve as temporary perches. They have two advantages: it provides a soft perch; the stripping of the bark is a game for the bird. Use horizontal, not vertical branches.

People using this type of perch should seek to obtain green branches and discard them when they become dry or stripped. The birds enjoy stripping the bark and sometimes will accomplish the task in 24 hours. Replacement might be required daily. The other advantage is that they provide a soft perch which is negated when the perch becomes hard and dry.

Equipment—Bird Bath

Every bird deserves and needs to bathe. (See Feather Care). The type of apparatus that you will need will vary almost with the individual bird.

SAUCER WITH WATER

Any type of low saucer or pan is adequate. The problems faced with this type of bathing is that the bird, through his splashing and shaking, will throw droplets of water into the surrounding area and pretty well wet it down. Containers can be purchased to hang on the door of the cage, which are shielded so that the moisture is kept within the birdbath. For birds that are allowed out of their cages, it is more convenient to let the bird bathe inside the confines of the kitchen sink.

One of the prerequisites for bird bathing is that it should be simple and not too much of a nuisance or problem for the bird owner. If it is easy to bathe the bird, chances are that it will get done. Otherwise, there is procrastination of this necessary function.

CARROT TOPS OR OTHER GREENS IN WHICH A BIRD WOULD DAMPEN HIS FEATHERS

In their native Australia, parakeets will walk through the grass which is wet from dew. Greens may be moistened and placed on the floor of the cage. If this is convenient for the owner, it will serve as a twin function of giving the bird his bath and supplying him with his greens for his daily dietary needs.

SHOWER

The small sprinkler, like the type used for watering houseplants, can be used to shower the bird. Some of the larger birds will enjoy getting into the regular shower bath for people, and some have accepted being sprayed by the attachment on the kitchen sink. One young man who has several parakeets moistens a washcloth and wrings it out over his birds. He claims that it is about as simple and easy a method to shower a bird that there is.

MIST

Although probably not as natural as other types of bathing, a mist produced from a regular plant mister of the home garden variety, works well on a bird. The mist is allowed to settle down over the bird, as most birds don't like to be squirted.

FOUNTAIN

For those people who have an aviary or a cage large enough to support a small fountain, it is a luxury for a bird. The bird is able to splash around in the water, yet be rained on at the same time.

Water and Seed Dishes

Feeding dishes need to be manufactured from material that can withstand cleaning and disinfection.

In the average home, the dishes should be able to be placed in the family automatic dishwasher.

To have a double set of dishes would be a nice convenience, allowing extra time for cleaning.

Aviculturalists will use either chemical disinfection or 180° heat.

Recreational Equipment

A cage would not be complete without some interesting toys or other playthings.

SWINGS

Standard swings are provided in most cages. A very interesting swing can be made from a string or rope. Loosely stretch the string from one side of the cage to the other, so the bird may rock to and fro, as a bird in the wild would land on a telephone wire.

PECK TOYS—SUCH AS DUMBBELLS AND BOUNCE BACK

The most common toy in this class and particularly to the parakeet one of the most valuable toys is a dumbbell. Parakeets become fascinated with these dumbbells. Possibly they accept the dumbbell as a friend or comrade and associate it with another bird.

MUSICAL TOYS—BELLS AND MUSICAL PERCHES

A bell qualifies as both a musical and reflection toy. Some birds enjoy the sound produced when they peck at it. The musical perch holds a fascination for birds and they use it frequently. The only disadvantage comes with the same tune being repeated over and over.

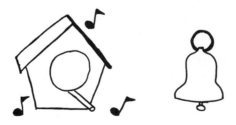

REFLECTION TOYS

   Mirrors, spoons, or any shiny object which might reflect an image fall into this category. The reflected image is the friendly face of another bird. It is the kind of acquaintance that has all the qualities that one would like to see in himself—hospitable, non-aggressive, devoted, intimate. The bird may sit in front of the mirror for long periods of time with such enrapture that he will seemingly almost forget everything else.

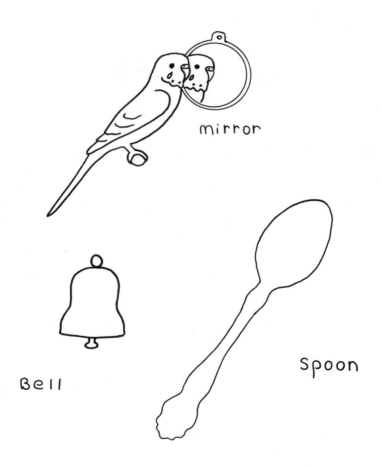

mirror

Bell

Spoon

CHEW TOYS SUCH AS: CORK, BONES, WOOD, BALLS, PAPER, FRESH BRANCHES, SPOOLS

Chewing is a natural quality in many birds. The curved beak of the psittacine family (all birds with a hooked bill) is meant for chewing.

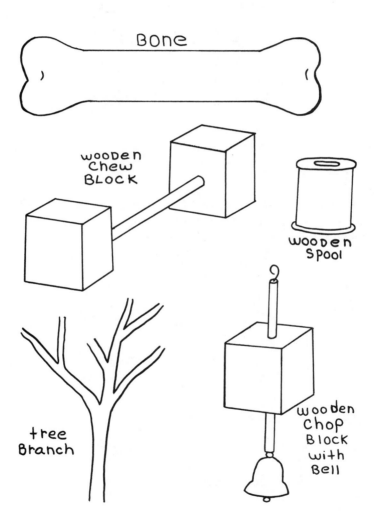

CLIMBING TOYS SUCH AS LADDERS, ROPES, CHAINS

The rope or chain can be hung from the top of the cage and can be anchored or free swinging.

PLAYGROUNDS

Commercially manufactured or home-made playgrounds consisting of swings, ladders, balls, jungle gyms, monkey bars and shallow ponds are interesting for the birds if enough room is available.

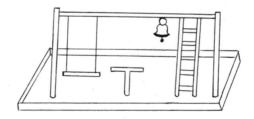

ACTION TOYS

Good examples of action toys are Merry-Go-Rounds, Ferris wheels, Elevators and Rocking toys.

38

HOLLOW TUBE TOYS

Playthings of this type are home made from an empty can or carton and hung from the top of the cage.

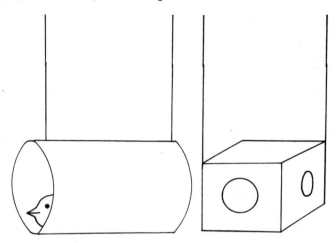

BITS AND PIECES

Soft billed birds may enjoy emptying containers filled with paper balls or other paraphernalia.

HANGING TOYS

Almost anything hung from the top of the cage might hold an interest for the bird. This includes bells, balls, boxes, keys, trapeze.

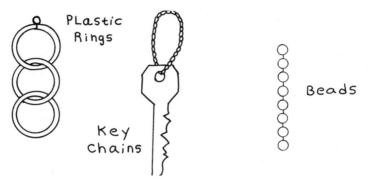

TOYS TO HIDE UNDER

Parakeets and some other birds enjoy hiding their heads.

PUZZLE TOYS

The psittacine bird with its agile tongue and tremendous control of its beak enjoys unlocking cage doors, removing val clamps from homemade cages or key chains.

Opening
key
chains

unlocking
cage door

PULL OUT TOYS

Plastic sticks inserted through a container can be removed by the bird.

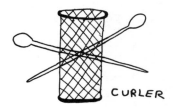

CURLER

BEAD TOYS

Beads hold a remarkable fascination for many birds.

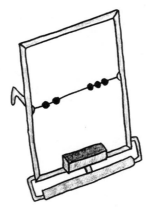

4 MENTAL ATTITUDE

The most magnificent, expensive, woodcarving in your home, no matter how celebrated and famous, could not become a companion to you. No oil painting, nor sculpture, nor any decoration in your home could ever appreciate you. It takes a living animal with a mentality to relate to others. This depends upon its capability, attitude and mental health.

In the course of an ordinary day those people working with birds see an assortment of personalities ranging from a nice average to both extremes of friendship and hostility. This reconfirms our knowledge that birds are emotional. Without feelings, there could be no fear, hostility or the opposite—friendly, outgoing, attention-seeking attitudes.

Influencing a bird's mental attitude and removing the fear of captivity is accomplished through proper caging, a pleasant environment, training, and becoming social.

Social Animals

Birds are social animals and require contact with other animals: birds, other pets and people. People are the most highly developed social species; friends, families, and social contacts are needed to maintain mental, and indirectly, physical health. Your pet bird is also a social animal and has requirements for friends, mates, and to act in a social order. Birds fly in flocks where there is community living, and taken away from all this and confined to isolation could gradually deteriorate in general health and eventually die.

A bird in your home learns to relate to you, and actually, when living in a caged situation, needs you for socialization. Talk to your bird; whistle to him; sing to him. He can't live well without you.

A bird is not equipped with the intelligence to know why we are happy or sad, but can feel the emotions of a human and can actually read this emotion as a hostile or friendly feeling.

A beautiful crested white cockatiel was imported into this country. He withstood the vigors of the thirty day quarantine and was sent to a reputable pet shop. The bird had areas on his body where he had begun to feather pick (pluck out feathers). At this point, the bird still looked good, but the owner of the pet shop, being conscientious, wanted to keep the bird until he was absolutely sure the feather picking had stopped. The feather picking did not cease; the bird continued picking until his chest and parts of his wings were becoming bare. Many attempts were made in the pet shop to overcome the problem. All were futile. A concerned lady had watched the bird in the pet shop for a period of four to six weeks, and had approached the pet shop owner many times about buying the bird. Finally, the deal was consummated wherein if the problem continued, she had the right to return the bird to the shop and receive her money back.

Her home was not the ordinary one; she had six active children with many friends constantly coming and going. Being a pet lover, she also had two dogs, another bird, and a guinea pig. She took the bird, put it in the middle of the family room, and within four weeks there was no feather picking at all and new feathers started growing in the bald areas.

The opposite could have happened, and the situation could have made the bird much worse. However, the bird gloried in his new social atmosphere, enjoyed the children and the attention he received from them, and, particularly, began to enjoy spoonfeeding by the husband.

The transition this bird made from the jungle to the private home is not unusual. Birds being a social animal adjust well to social situations, as long as we remember they are living things with feelings and emotions and sensitivities.

Proper Caging

Proper caging helps to relax a bird and remove the fear of captivity. When the bird feels safe, he will feel confortable in your presence. It is only when a bird has this confidence that it will accept gestures of kindness and friendship from the owner.

The cage might have to be redesigned several times or tried in various rooms in the house before the right combination of security and environment is reached. See section on Bird Cages.

Playing

Playing seems to be a very natural behavior in birds, as likewise it is for other animals, especially the young. A parakeet performing sommersaults while hanging onto the bars at the side of the cage seems to be performing tricks for his own amusement. Canaries are seen rocking back and forth on their swings as a fun time. Parrots will amuse themselves by hanging upside down from the top of the cage, cocking their head from one side to the other or be very busy stripping the bark off a green stick. All of these activities seem to enrich the bird's life and seem to be an expression of contentment and happy attitude.

Basically, a bird must be healthy to even begin to participate in these types of actions. If your bird doesn't play, it may be that he is not feeling well and should be checked by a veterinarian.

Toys

Toys have been covered in more detail under the section on Cage Equipment.

Free Flying

Birds that can participate in free flying will find it an excellent type of recreation, and it will benefit the bird both physically and mentally.

Bathing

Birds seem to enjoy a bath or shower and therefore this is included under recreation although there are many more advantages than just this. Birds look forward to and enjoy their baths and the amusement involved.

Companionship

Birds need a friend to relate to. This friend could be another bird or it could be a person who is supplying the necessary social stimulation.

Two birds really don't ever play together but do provide companionship for each other.

Communication

Another fact of the social life of a bird is communication. For any animal, there cannot be social life without methods of communication. When a bird sings or sends a message, and there is an answer, we acknowledge this social stimulation. If we listen to a number of birds, we will detect quite a variety of sounds, and it will seem to us, although unintel-

47

ligible, as if some sort of talking is taking place. Birds, in fact, communicate more messages and have larger vocabularies than any other animals. Dogs and cats have very limited vocabularies. Birds express alarm, distress, aggressiveness, call a group together, announce a source of food, and make appropriate vocal responses to a member of the opposite sex.

There are methods of communication other than sound and birds use these also. Much time has been spent in learning to interpret the gestures and postures of birds. Through their actions they can show aggressiveness and appeasement. Gestures are important in courtship and include various motions of the head and tail or display of conspicuous plumage.

Birds communicate by way of sounds that are not vocal. These include flying sounds made with their wings. The sound of wings on takeoff constitute signals of some sort. The other type of nonvocal sounds are tapping and snapping the beak. Cockatiels are one common pet bird that occasionally make a knocking sound with the beak. To return the knocking sound seems to stimulate him to do it further. Toucans will make a hollow, clicking sound with their beak that can be a signal of distress or a cry for food.

It is interesting to see how well birds learn to communicate with their masters. Birds are known to call their masters' names when they feel they want attention or food.

Friendship and Training

No attempt to start training should be made until two things have been accomplished. First, the bird must feel comfortable and secure in his environment. This is discussed under Caging. Second, a friendly relationship and the beginning of a mutual trust must be established. But how does the bird know that you want to be his friend? He can't understand English and your antics and gestures may upset him more than accomplishing what you want. How do you communicate your friendly wishes to your bird?

48

A combination of hand feeding on your part and a little hunger on the bird's part will help cross the social barrier faster than anything else. Feed your bird twice daily and between meals take his food away. By feeding at about 12-hour intervals, the bird begins to look forward to mealtime because of hunger. It won't be long before the bird realizes where his food comes from and who is feeding him. This makes the bird come to you.

Once the bird is coming to you, the next step becomes hand feeding— and so on.

Food is the reward to be used any time a satisfactory word is said or trick is accomplished. Training in this manner accomplishes nice things in a positive manner.

Never hit your bird unless you purposely feel that you need to make him afraid of you. Your bird remembers your attitudes and your actions. Nature seems to have built in a defense mechanism whereby unpleasant or harmful incidents are long retained.

5 ENVIRONMENT

The Bird's Surroundings

In a discussion of a bird's environment, consideration must be given to the cage, the surroundings, and all activities in that area. The bird's house is his cage, but his home includes practically everything else. For the bird to function properly and become an asset to his owner, he has to live in a pleasant environment.

Temperature

Although feathers have a variety of functions, the chief of these is heat conservation. Small birds with their small bodies loose their body heat much more rapidly than the large birds. As a result of this, you will notice nature has given finches and canaries a much denser feather covering than larger birds.

There is one canary breeder who keeps his birds in his attic. He claims that occasionally in the winter time he will have to knock the ice off the water before his birds can drink, yet his birds are tremendously healthy. This example is *extreme*, but is given to indicate that our birds can tolerate cold as long as they are healthy and well fed.

Most birds even of the tropical variety are wearing a very expensive down jacket which is covered with contour feathers comparable to a nylon windbreaker. Therefore, a 10 or 20 degree change in the temperature of your home should not appreciably bother your bird—if he is healthy. A sick bird or one in marginal health will chill from this change in temperature and could even die.

If the bird in your house is bothered by the coolness of the air conditioning in the summer time then move him to a warm room and seek a diagnosis.

Drafts

Drafts in your home which do not bother you should not be any problem to a bird. It is not common sense to set a bird cage directly in front of any air conditioner nor would you want to obviously put him in an area where there is a cold draft. In the average home, drafts will likely be a minimal problem.

Heat

Heat may be a bigger problem to some birds than the cold. In the example of the man who kept his birds in the attic during the winter time, he would very likely have those birds die because of the heat in his attic in the summertime. Birds left in the hot sun on a summer day will die of being overheated.

Humidity

An ideal humidity seems to be 40–50%, although a humidity much lower than this is well tolerated except in breeding conditions. The dry brittle feather associated with very dry air has not been reported in household situations.

Clean Air

The spectacular, efficient respiratory system of the bird requires pure air flowing through the lungs, air sacs and sinuses. Unfortunately, nature didn't provide a filter designed to cope with all the modern air pollution. To contaminate this system with smoke, dust, volatile chemicals leads to problems including death.

Air Pollution

Location of Cage

An area of family activity which provides the bird with the most socialization is probably the best place to keep him. In most homes the kitchen or the recreation room is the happiest place for the bird. There has been some suggestion that a gas range could give off noxious gases which would injure a bird, but I have never found this to be true. It is possible that this was true many years ago. The opposite situation should be mentioned here. Could the bird in the kitchen be a threat to the owner's health? The answer is no. Rarely could anything be transmitted from your bird to you. There is much more risk just walking down the street than there is to catching something from your pet bird, although it always pays to be precautious. If you are suspicious that your bird is sick, it should be seen by a veterinarian.

Outside walls, depending upon the temperature and amount of insulation, may cause undue exposure to cold. Drafts that are tolerated by us generally don't bother a bird.

The Lake Michigan waterfront in Chicago is especially beautiful, and Mrs. Jones, who had a parakeet which had become particularly endeared to here, wanted her bird to enjoy the view. She has always lived in an apartment several blocks from the lakefront and now had the opportunity to rent one with a picture window facing the lake. Upon moving she carefully arranged the furniture so that the bird cage could be directly in front of the large picture window. Unfortunately, the bird could not tolerate the amount of light, became psychologically and neurologically upset. After consultation with the doctor, he was put in a dark bedroom during the day. Even over a period of time the bird could not adjust to the picture windows.

Animals, including people, become accustomed to a "status quo" routine and a very organized life. A variance from this can be upsetting and cause an internal turmoil which is reflected externally. How does this apply to birds? As strange as it may seem, a bird can become accustomed to living in one room or even become accustomed to the arrangement of the furniture. Changing things can fluster the bird. Most of the time they readjust quickly, and the temporary upset is not noticed by the owner. Of course, the bird that is not readjusting must be moved back to his familiar surroundings.

In the organized order of things, birds can become used to being fed, having their paper changed, and receiving attention at a certain time of the day. When this varies, they can become upset.

As we are living close to a bird, and begin to have a feeling for him, we will learn to recognize these situations and help the bird through them.

Photoperiods—A Bird Is a Slave to Light

Many effects can be had by shortening and lengthening the amount of light that the bird receives in 24 hours. Poultry raisers for years have stimulated increased egg production by having the lights in their poultry houses remain on extra hours after sunset. For centuries the Japanese have forced caged birds to sing in midwinter by lengthening their days by candlelight for 3 to 4 hours after sunset in the fall. Birds' migration is partially based on the number of hours of light there is and, conversely, the number of hours of darkness that there is in a day.

Pet birds probably require the same amount of light and dark that are occurring in a natural day. In the summer the bird would have eight hours of darkness daily and in the winter they would have about 12 hours of darkness daily. The periods of light and dark are controlled in pet birds with a heavy cage cover.

The bird in the family recreation room who is kept up until midnight every night because of the television programs and who then has his sleep cut short in the morning because the sun rises early or a light is turned on may be receiving only 5 or 6 hours of sleep every day. Inadequate amounts of rest for the bird will cause constant stress and eventually will show the result of this strain in a breakdown of their health.

Music

Canaries that hear other canaries singing on a record or over the radio return the song in a lively manner. Cockatiels are known to enjoy the beat and the sound of music and squawk and cluck as long as they hear it and stop when the music stops. They seem to enjoy making sounds with the music and it is to be encouraged.

6 FACTS and CARE: BEAK and NAILS

Because of its position on the end of a long and flexible neck, the bird's beak serves not only as the beginning of the alimentary canal, but also as a hand. A list of functions ascribed to the beak testify to its usefulness.

Beside the obvious need for the beak to be involved in food gathering, holding, transporting and preparing (hulling and splitting) seeds are the following functions:

Pincers or tongs for getting into small areas
Grooming and preening
Defense and combat
Courtship
Making nests and turning eggs
Feeding the young
Noises—clattering and snapping
Climbing

Functions assigned to the beak make it responsible for much of the health of the bird. The beak requires proper care, and in the pet bird should be attended to regularly.

It would be easy to surmise that the beak is composed of solid bone, and if you saw a parrot crack a large seed that would require a man with a hammer to open, you would be convinced. The structure of the beak is well-designed for the bird's needs, but it is not indestructible. When the beak is used for the purposes designed, such as cracking seed, removing the shell, and for other purposes listed, it serves the bird well. Unnatural forces applied to the beak may split and crack it.

The beak consists of a relatively thin, horny covering over a hard, bony structure. This outer horny covering or coreum is made up of material similar to the horns or antlers of other wild animals, and its normal appearance in birds should be smooth and uniform in color and texture. The coreum grows continuously, but the rate of growth varies in different species of birds.

Rate of Growth of Upper Beak (Approximate)

Canary	$1\frac{1}{3}$ to $1\frac{1}{2}''$ per year
Budgerigar (parakeet)	$3''$ per year
Parrot	$1\frac{1}{4}''$ per year

The lower beak grows at a slightly slower rate.

If the tissue beneath the coreum were solid bone, the weight of the beak in a bird as large as a parrot could upset his sense of balance and equilibrium. Instead, the bony portion is porous and the center is hollow (pneumatic) connecting with the respiratory system. In spite of being porous, the bony structure is hard and gives the beak its shape and strength.

Members of the parrot family have an upper hooked beak which extends over the lower beak. In many of these birds, one-third of the total length of the beak projects over the lower beak.

The interaction of the upper and lower beaks helps keep the length normal. The lower beak wears off the upper beak, and at the same time, is being worn down. Anything that interferes with normal beak and mouth activity allows for overgrowth of beaks.

56

Normal beaks

57

Normal Use of Beak in Parrot

The awesome hooked beak of the members of the parrot family have been designed primarily for cracking, splitting and some chewing. An average size parrot will take a rib-bone, chip away at it until he uncovers the marrow, and then eat it. They can take nuts and crack the shell with relative ease and eat the meat out of the center. Folks who have housed their bird in a not-too-well-constructed cage have witnessed a parrot bending the bars, removing the clips that hinge the doors, and breaking the welds. Perches made from pine are easily split and are a toy for as short as 24 hours. These birds are not to be discouraged from chewing, but in fact, should be supplied with bones, branches from trees, pieces of wood upon which they can exercise and wear down the beak in a normal manner, in the way nature prescribed.

When a parrot takes a nut in his mouth, he holds it with his tongue and upper beak and then through the movements of his lower jaw, shreds and grates off the nut until it drops to the bottom of the cage in sawdust like pieces. Sometimes he eats the nut, and many times he uses this as an exercise. If you examine the underside of the hooked beak, you would find that there are a series of ridges, sometimes in an unusual design, that act as a rasp and serve to hold any material pressed against it. The bird uses these ridges when holding nuts with his tongue and grinding them with his lower jaw.

Beware of Overgrown Beaks

An overgrown beak may be a warning sign that the bird's vitality has decreased due to an illness. Some of the hardest diseases to recognize are those which gradually develop, and the main sign of a problem is decreased activity. Birds are experts at hiding their problems, and slight clues are sometimes the only apparent things we have to judge their health.

It is possible the bird owner will bring a bird to a pet shop or veterinarian for a beak trim, and the bird will die while being held for the procedure. The customer thinks the very worst, becomes irate, believing the bird was killed because of wreckless or inept handling. What else can he believe? He thought he had a healthy bird, and now it is dead.

Any time a beak overgrows, the cause should be established. The source of the problem could be minor, but even then a physical examination by a veterinarian and an evaluation of the situation is warranted.

After the trauma of the loss of a pet, no amount of explanation will help. Even an autopsy with actual demonstration of the pathological lesion might not be convincing. Careful questioning will uncover some sign of deterioration—less activity, feathers ruffled more often, singing or talking less or not at all, and gradual weight loss.

Don't wait for the problems caused by such an incident. Stay ahead of trouble by being aware of the warning sign of overgrown beaks.

Care to Prevent Beak Problems

In the explanations of the normal beak, emphasis was placed on its structure and rate of growth. If these facts are understood, along with an appreciation for the importance of the beak, these recommendations will fall into place naturally. Of course, a healthy beak requires a healthy body and a completely balanced diet. These are basic to any other consideration.

The first duty is to allow the beak to function in its normal manner as prescribed by nature.

The *soft billed birds* primarily use their beaks for gathering, holding, transporting and preparing food, grooming and preening, and pecking in the soil and other areas to obtain minerals and grit. All of these tasks are fulfilled for caged birds with the following:

Chewing work for the beak:
   Hulling seed
   Splitting or breaking food
   Stripping and chewing on greens or branches
Encouraging normal grooming and preening
Applying cuttlebone, mineral blocks or a grit-mineral mixture for normal pecking

Providing a hard perch or other object to augment the normal beak
rubbing and cleaning actions

Despite these measures, the beak may have to be trimmed at 3–6
month intervals. Since this procedure will likely be performed infrequent-
ly, someone who is familiar should perform the beak trimming; such as
the pet shop, a bird breeder, an animal technician, or a veterinarian.

The *parrot family* use their beaks mainly in handling and hulling seed,
grooming and preening, grasping and splitting hard material, rubbing
beak and climbing. To aid in the useful function of the beak, provide the
following:

Chewing work for the beak:
Seed to crack and hull
Nuts in their shell to crack and hull—proportional to the size of the
bird's mouth
Biscuits to chew on—hard dog biscuits can be used for this
Bones—many parrots seem to enjoy working on small bones to get
at the marrow
Branches from shrubs or trees (non-toxic, edible type). Birds will
strip the bark off and then chew on the branch
Hang toys which are suspended from the roof of the cage. Nylon
bones or other similar objects invite the birds to chew and handle
Cuttlebone, mineral block or a mineral-salt-grit mixture

A hard perch or other object to rub and clean the beak.
Climb toys—chains or other hang toys to exercise the beak in climbing.

Some birds, as they become older, develop a problem in which the
normal contour of the beak changes. Because of these distortions, the
upper and lower beak do not mesh properly, and thus, lose the beneficial
effect of the beak wearing off from their interactions. This situation is
most frequently seen in budgerigars. The bird is normal at birth with the
beak having the proper alignment and occlusion. A slight loss of angle
puts the upper beak beyong the reach of the lower beak. The upper
beak, which originally was about a quarter circle, begins to straighten,

and in the extreme case, resembles a duck beak. Without the normal wearing off of the upper beak, it lengthens one-fourth inch a month or three inches a year. These beaks, therefore, need to be trimmed every four weeks or the lengthened beak will interfere with normal eating. The lower beak is generally not affected and continues to wear away in a normal manner. However, the lower beak should be observed, as cases have occurred where it needed trimming.

Procedure for Beak Trimming

Christmas toys frequently can be assembled without reading the instructions, but before attempting procedures on your bird, knowing exactly the proper technique and the types of problems you might encounter makes good sense. Better yet, watch the procedure performed by a good teacher; do it yourself under his guidance; discuss the technique thoroughly with all the problems that can be involved doing it. Then you are probably competent to handle 80–90% of the cases of birds needing beak trims.

PATTERNS

Other birds of the same species are the best models to follow.

Pictures of normal birds can be used as guides.

If the beak were divided lengthwise, each half should be exactly the same. When the two halves do not match, correction is probably needed.

The normal half will serve as an immediate pattern for the opposite side.

BLEEDING—Be prepared to take steps to control bleeding. (See section on Bleeding.)

UNDERSTAND THE PROPER METHOD OF CATCHING A BIRD AND THEN THE CORRECT METHOD OF RESTRAINT

PROPER EQUIPMENT

Special scissors and clippers are available at pet shops.

For use on small birds, regular manicure equipment is adequate.

TECHNIQUE—For small birds, trimming off the tip of the beak presents relatively few problems. Upon catching the bird, hold the head securely and clip off just a little less than you intended. Trimming will be needed repeatedly every 3–4 months. Even though the beak of a canary will grow ⅛" or about 2 millimeters every month, ordinary daily wear will keep the beak from needing attention for 2–4 months. The beak of a budgerigar grows more rapidly and will need attention about every 4–5 weeks.

Large birds are less prone to overgrown beaks than the small birds. Before trimming beaks on a parrot, be certain it is abnormal. More commonly than overgrowth are beaks that do not wear evenly due to either the upper or lower beaks being slightly off mid-line. The sides of the beak will thicken and need to be pared down to their normal size and shape. By reshaping the opposing beaks more normal wear between the beaks in re-established. Since the malocclusion cannot be corrected, reshaping of the beak will be required every 3–6 months.

Any time a beak is being trimmed, there is a danger that the beak will be split or the jaw fractured. Because of the problems in handling large birds and their strength and ability to move suddenly, extra care is needed to prevent this type of accident.

Nail Trimming

No rule of thumb will solve the riddle of the proper amount to trim off a toe nail. Only experience can guide you. The quick on many nails (the fleshy core of the nail) reaches further toward the tip than might be expected. In order to avoid cutting deep into the quick, the nail should be trimmed off a small amount at a time. By this procedure if the quick happens to be cut, the bleeding should be minor.

It is better to trim the nails and cope with a bleeding problem than to let the nails overgrow.

Procedure to Control Bleeding from the Beak or Toenails

BLOOD SEEPING SLOWLY

Small blood vessels reach toward the tip of the beak and nail and are unavoidably cut at times. These ordinarily pose no problem and control of bleeding is managed by applying a powder (starch, baking soda, boric acid), pressing it against the wound, and holding the powder in place for ten seconds. If needed, repeat once or several times. After returning the bird to the cage, the nail should be observed for a few minutes. At times when the bird grasps the perch, the nail will start rebleeding.

SLOW CONTINUOUS BLEEDING

If it is obvious that simple treatment will not stop the bleeding, or if simple treatment has not been successful, then a combination of chemical cautery and direct pressure is needed. Of the available chemical cauteriz-

ing agents, the two most common are silver nitrate and Monsels powder (iron sub-sulfate). (At times, corn starch or baking power will work just as well.) The Monsels powder, which seems to have the advantage, is pressed directly onto the bleeding surface and then held for 3–5 minutes. At times, the blood will come up through the Monsels powder and a fresh application will be needed. The Monsels powder may be used generously and, combined with direct pressure, will control most bleeding. The powder should be applied with your fingers, and the direct pressure is also with your fingers. The 3–5 minutes holding may seem an unusually long time, but blood clotting in a bird is sometimes very slow, the body must be given a chance to develop a firm clot. It the Monsels powder is being applied to the beak, avoid allowing the bird to swallow any.

Bleeding of this type is potentially serious. This bird should be watched carefully for 30–60 minutes to be sure that the bleeding does not start again. If the shock of the handling has bothered the bird, place it for an hour in a cage heated to 80–85 degrees.

HEAVY BLEEDING

The third step in controlling hemorrhage is only to be used when treatment with chemical cauterizing agents and direct pressure has been diligently used and failed. Very seldom is this drastic a treatment needed, but bleeding must be controlled. Coagulation of a cut surface by heat is only intended to be used on a very limited area when bleeding cannot be controlled with other methods. In the case of a beak or toenail, the bleeding surface is small, so that it can be seared with a red-hot needle. The needle is flamed until glowing red, then touched to the bleeding surface. At times, this may have to be supplemented with Monsels powder and direct pressure.

If the bird shows any degree of shock, it should be put in a cage heated to 80 or 85 degrees and kept in a completely dark area to limit its activity. Since there is the danger of rebleeding from the cut surface, any type of activity might loosen the clot and allow hemorrhage to start. In a completely black area, the bird ordinarily will be immobile. The bird should be kept under these conditions for 1–2 hours, but observed intermittently during this time.

Prolonged bleeding could cause shock and death. The veterinarian should be called in these cases.

7 FACTS and CARE: EYE and EAR

The list of unusual and remarkable qualities of a bird includes its colorful feathering, its song, graceful nature, and flying ability—and yet—one of its most stunning attributes is its eyes. The eyes of a bird have reached the state of perfection, superior to that of any other animal. This advanced state allows the bird to visually obtain more information about its surroundings than available to any other living thing. The eye collects data about the direction, distance, size, shape, color, three dimensional depth, and motion of an object. Whether this be an enemy or a food source, the bird has an advantage.

To perform the function nature has assigned, a large eye is required. For its size, a bird has enormous eyes, although the mass stays hidden in the skull. The eyelids open to expose only that small part of the eye (cornea) needed to allow entrance of light. So while the eye externally appears small, the opposite condition exists.

Birds have three eyelids—an outer upper and lower lid and the third eyelid just inside the others. The third eyelid (membrance nictatans) performs the job of cleaning and moistening the cornea. The inner surface is covered with cells which possess brushlike processes, so that the cornea is painted with tears at every blink. In addition, it cleans the undersurface of the eyelid on the return journey of each sweep, much like a windshield wiper. Pet birds blink with their third eyelid 30–60 times a minute, and sometimes so swiftly as to be almost undetected. A large gland under the third eyelid furnishes much of the lubrication for the eye.

Normal eye—note eye lashes

The upper and lower lid protects the eye and closes when the bird is sleeping. If the upper and lower lids are closed in a "sleepy" fashion, especially in an active environment, it can be a reliable sign of sickness.

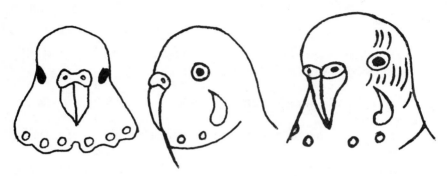

A bird sees you from many angles.

Care of the Eyes

Besides being unusual, the bird's eyes are exceptionally resistant to some of the problems seen in mammals. Local infections, such as conjunctivitis, are unusual, but when troubles do appear, they are much more serious and difficult.

SIGNS OF EYE PROBLEMS INCLUDE

Swollen or bulging eyes
Eyelids thickened or held completely or partially closed
Loss of feathers around the eyes
Rubbing eyes on perch or other object and scratching them with their claws
Discharge of any type
Loss of vision—lids may be pasted shut
Blinking more than usual

67

Infection may be missed because the bird usually turns his healthy eye in the direction of the observer.

FIRST AID

Eye problems should be treated by a veterinarian as soon as possible. Until assistance can be obtained:

Keep eye warm and avoid chilling. The cage temperature should be raised to 85°

Wash eye with any eye antiseptic manufactured either for birds or humans.

If the bird is scratching at his eye or face with his claws, apply emergency Elizabethan collar.

The condition may be contagious, and strict isolation is recommended.

If the bird's eyes are closed, death from starvation may result. The lids can be bathed open with any warm eye antiseptic.

By rubbing the infected eye on the perches, the discharge may contaminate the perches. Careful cleaning and disinfection with regular changes of perches is necessary.

Ear

Hearing is apparently well-developed in all birds. The fact that they communicate by voice shows this. The way songbirds and parrots imitate sounds prove that they hear them the same way we do.

The bird's hearing covers about the same sound range as man. It has been suggested that due to the broader construction of the hearing mechanism, birds are less sensitive to a wide range of sound frequencies than mammals but more sensitive to differences in intensity. Further, a bird is able to hear and respond to rapid fluctuations in song about ten times as rapidly as man can.

The ear, besides its importance in hearing, is the organ of equilibrium. The basic structure of the inner ear reached such a high state of perfection, even in fishes, that its basic design has remained unchanged up the evolutionary ladder all the way to mammals.

The ear of a bird is not apparent because it has no external pinna (ear flap). Feathers hide the ear in all of our pet birds. To locate the ear, the feathers must be parted in the area below and in back of the eye. The ear at this point is merely a tube that carries sound waves from the surrounding air inward to the ear drum at its base. The wall of the outer ear canal may contain a number of small sebaceous glands. The ear glands secrete wax, but seldom is a buildup noticeable.

Recommendation: An infection, parasites, accumulation of wax or other abnormality would be signaled by a loss of feathers or the bird's rubbing the side of his head. These symptoms or any head tilt should be seen by your veterinarian.

8 FACTS and CARE: FEATHERS

Feather Facts

Feathers cannot in any way be compared to hair, and indeed, are so completely different, that the first requirement is to learn and understand some basic facts about them.

Soon after birth, every bird is presented with an expensive down-lined jacket that is carefully fitted to cover his entire body except for his feet and legs and parts of his face. The down is a special material that is guaranteed to be light and fluffy. The down in this jacket is, likewise, guaranteed to keep the body warm in cold weather and is adjustable to keep the body comfortable in warm weather. This special coat has an outer covering of contour feathers that the designer has made beautiful as well as functional. When the wind blows, it serves as an excellent windbreaker; when it rains, the jacket is waterproof. The thickness and strength of this coat protect the body thermally and mechanically. Besides all this, the bird is given a magic carpet which is a marvel of engineering design. The flight feathers on the wings are strong and flexible, which gives the bird flight whenever he wants it.

The key to water repellancy of feathers is the feather structure and feather network, not the natural oil. The micro-structure of the wide flat part of feathers involves interlocking barbules that may number up to one million in a single feather. This zipper effect gives strength to the web, but also traps air, helping to make the feather water tight.

Feathers grow only in special patches or tracts, with intervening featherless spaces.

Feather coloring is the result of a combination of pigments and light refraction.

Lubrication of feathers decreases wear and is the function of the preening gland and powder down.

The preening or uropygial gland secretes an oil which the bird spreads with its beak onto its feathers and claws. In the pet bird class, some of the psittacines lack a uropygial gland.

Disintegration of the tips of powder down feathers produces a fine powder that helps to waterproof, lubricate, and preserve the feathers.

A bird's feathers must be replaced before they become worn out. The annual molt, replacing old feathers with new ones, is a dangerous time in the bird's life, since the expenditure of energy to replace its feathers leaves the bird vulnerable to illness.

The feather follicle normally begins to grow a new feather as soon as the quill of the old feather is removed. Within two weeks, the feather is one fourth to one half inch long.

Preening for a bird is more important than is hair grooming for a person, and it should be encouraged. Birds preen their feathers continuously but at irregular intervals. Stress will cause a bird to alter its preening habits.

Birds maintain their feathers by means of a number of different types of baths: splashing in a pool of water, showers, dust baths, sun baths, swimming and walking through wet greens.

Complete feather care cannot be accomplished unless the bird is healthy both mentally and physically. Mental health demands companionship, a pleasant environment and security from stress. Physical health is related to a balanced diet, good sanitation and housing, and control of diseases.

A Time for Special Care—Molting

In return for the many months' happiness that our bird gives us, he needs special care during molting. If people went through a molt or similar situation, we could appreciate the physical and mental stress. However, no comparable situation exists.

Molting is a primary factor in a bird's life and must proceed without a snag. The pitfalls of a difficult molt extend from minor delays to chilling and death. Nature has timed the molting cycle to occur under the most ideal conditions. Rarely does an event in the life of an animal occur where the environment becomes so involved with an internal process that intertwines nourishment, nutritional reserves, the endocrine (hormone) system, the circulatory system and the integumentary system. Nature provides warmth, rain, humidity, lengthening photoperiods, and a luxurious food supply. The bird must provide a good healthy body, having its reserves prepared and its hormone system tuned to undertake a molt. The countdown starts when spring arrives. Molting starts after the reproductive cycle.

RECOMMENDATIONS FOR ANY BIRD IN A MOLT

HEAT—In a normal molt, no area of the bird's body ever loses all its feathers. However, the feathering is definitely thin, and this may cause the bird to chill. To avoid this, the room temperature should not be allowed to drop. Should the bird's feathers become ruffled, the room temperature should be raised. If this is not successful, the bird should be placed in an incubator, with the temperature elevated and maintained at about 80° F. A homemade incubator may be prepared by placing a heating pad alongside the cage and wrapping the cage with a plastic wrap. An opening for ventilation is made at the cage door. It is desirable to maintain the heat until the molt is complete. Depending upon the quality of the molt, this could continue longer than eight weeks. Remember, the bird with the abnormal molt will require the longest care and nursing.

REST—Eight to twelve hours of total darkness per day will be required during the annual molt.

SECURITY—Feather picking and other vices are more apt to begin during the molting period. With all the bird's energy being used to grow new feathers and with the loss of some flight and tail feathers, its instincts render it more susceptible to predatory animals. Confinement in an open cage enhances its fears and creates emotional problems, manifested as feather picking and hostility.

QUIET—In nature, a molting bird resides in a peaceful, safe area. Molting pet birds should be kept in an area free of disturbances.

PREENING—As the molting process begins, the bird becomes increasingly concerned with its plumage. When the quills begin to loosen, the bird removes them and is then ready to care for the new feathers. Each new feather is wrapped in a protective keratin casing. As the feather grows in length, this sheath must be removed before it can open. (The sheath is like a cover on an umbrella—the umbrella cannot be opened until the cover has been removed.) After the bird removes the protective coating the feather is still curled and the vein (flat part) is narrow. Preening flattens the feather and opens it to its full width.

With hundreds of new feathers regenerating, the bird must preen constantly. A white flaky material resulting from the bird's preening will collect on the cage paper and may alarm the owner, because it resembles heavy dandruff. Coupled with intense preening, it will cause some owners to think that the bird has dry, flaky, itchy skin. A natural but erroneous conclusion would be that oil is needed on the bird's skin and feathers. However, this powder is simply the residue of the keratin sheath, which the bird removes from around the feather, a normal and desirable process.

BATHING—For many birds, bathing is a refreshing experience that encourages preening. A bath to some birds is splashing in a dish of water; to others, it is being "rained on" or rolling in wet greens.

LUXURIOUS FOOD SUPPLY—To supply the bird with a variety of food is relatively easy; to assure that the bird eats a variety of food can be quite difficult. Molting is a test of the adequacy of the bird's nutritional

73

state. Nutritional deficiencies are exposed probably more often during molting than at any other time of the bird's life. A specific molting food does not exist, and if the owner waits until a molt to feed the bird a balanced diet, there will be problems. An owner should add egg to the bird's diet during the molting period. The eggs can be prepared so that they are appetizing to the bird or may be included in other foods, such as egg biscuits, pound cake, or cookies with a high egg content.

Controlling Flight

Controlling flight by clipping or plucking flight feathers is a subject which should be talked over with the pet shop or veterinarian.

Ruffled Feathers

Conserving body heat is the most important function of feathers. The greater the thickness of the feathers, the better the insulation around the bird. Ruffled feathers signal that a pet bird is chilled and has a real need for heat. Birds chill under adverse conditions, either when the ambient temperature is very low or when the bird is ill.

A bird that is ill and cold is also hungry. Ruffled feathers in a pet bird are a warning sign and should be attended to; if not, the bird will soon die. Ruffled feathers are not a sign of a feather problem; they function as a body defense mechanism against chilling.

Feather Picking

Feather picking is primarily a disease of confinement and results from stress and poor husbandry. Feather mites may be a cause, but this possibility should be ruled out during the veterinarian's examination.

The stress of captivity is based on one factor—insecurity. A bird feels safe only when it can immediately fly away from any disturbance and then hide in a sheltered area. Birds can become very fearful when caged, and unless they can establish a protected area, they are apt to begin to act unnaturally. These birds are described as being somewhat nervous, unfriendly, apprehensive and introverted. Before the feather picking vice is initiated, the bird will lessen its normal preening habits and gradually substitute feather chewing. A common cause of picking is the added tension the bird experiences during a molt. The bird's instincts direct it to increase preening with gentle handling of the feathers, but because of its mental state, it reacts violently—chewing, picking and plucking them.

Other stressful situations that may induce feather picking include isolation from other birds or limited contact with people, since birds are social animals and need companionship; insufficient rest (lack of darkness); malnutrition; fright from many sources, including noise; and close confinement.

Feather picking would not be a problem (1) if bird cages were designed to provide a place for concealment; (2) if birds had an owner or another bird as a companion; and (3) if good basic husbandry practices were followed, which includes providing a balanced diet, 8 to 12 hours of darkness, frequent baths and protection against agitating situations.

Bathing

When you are going to wear your shirt day and night for a year, it makes sense to take good care of it. Birds are faced with just that problem and thus take every opportunity to maintain themselves in excellent condition.

Bathing is an important part of total feather care, and the bird should be allowed (or sometimes forced) to carry on this normal function. Not all birds bathe in the same manner so a number of approaches are taken. (See Section on Bathing Equipment.)

9 FACTS and CARE: RESPIRATORY SYSTEM

The importance of maintaining a healthy respiratory system and the need to recognize any slight abnormality immediately cannot be overemphasized. The avian respiratory system is the most intricate and efficient of any vertebrate: a complex, sophisticated system developed over millions of years through the evolutionary process which selected for light weight and a method to oxygenate the blood for sustained flights over great distances. Large air sacs and hollow bones connect to a lung which always stays expanded and has air constantly circulating through it. The total volume of the respiratory system occupies up to 20% of the total body mass. This large organ system is particularly susceptible to infection, and thus, requiring added surveillance and care.

Respiratory problems of pet birds are characterized by their slow, sneaky onset, and then their persistence to the point that the life of the animal may be endangered. Unlike typical respiratory problems of man (colds), which are self limiting and rarely are serious or have complications, the respiratory problems of pet birds must be considered potentially dangerous. *If the initial respiratory infection doesn't kill the patient, there is a possibility that the complications and after-effects will.* The conclusion to be drawn from these statements is that the pet bird owner should be alert for the earliest signs of a problem and then start treatment immediately. If respiratory diseases are not "put out" early, they can become deeply entrenched and difficult to treat. After these diseases become established, complications and after-effects occur.

Signs of Respiratory Problems

SNEEZING

Much information can be gained about the respiratory system by simply listening and watching. Unless you are an excellent observer and a keen listener, you probably have never heard a bird sneeze.

Sneezing is thought of in terms of our own experience. A person who is about to sneeze "winds up" with a deep inspiration, and then follows with a forceful noisy explosion of air out of the nose and mouth. Head movements and blinking of the eyes accompany this reflex.

comparative problems

Almost the opposite takes place with a sneezing bird. The sound produced would not attract any unusual attention. It could easily be overlooked as a normal sound, as it is soft and fast. In a room with moderate noise, it would never be heard. The bird's sneeze generates a sound somewhat similar to that of a noise made when a person snaps his moistened lips by gently blowing through them. Head movements and respiratory discharge are hardly detectable.

Sneezing occurs when there is an irritation deep in the nasal passage. It functions as a defense reflex mechanism to eliminate foreign material from the nose. The force of the sneeze aids in cleaning the nose.

Sneezing can always be considered a sign of a problem, and steps should be taken to remove the irritant, be it airborne or disease. Even though the sneeze of a bird is hardly noticeable, don't overlook this dependable sign.

NASAL DISCHARGE

A discharge collecting in the nares, on the feathers above the nares, or on the beak is prime evidence of a respiratory infection.

comparative problems

"Runny" nose

The feathers are stained dark due to a nasal discharge.

COUGHING

Coughs in birds sound like "clicks," "chirping" and "clucks." It would be much better for the bird if the cough was loud and raucous. Attention would then be directed to the problem especially if the bird kept his owner awake all night due to the coughing. Just as with sneezes, it takes a trained ear to understand that it is abnormal. Always consider it serious.

comparative problems

LOSS OR CHANGE OF VOICE

A canary that sings hoarse or off-key is just as abnormal as an out-of-tune piano. Generally, it isn't that the bird needs singing lessons or needs to be taught new lyrics. The problem is inflammation or infection.

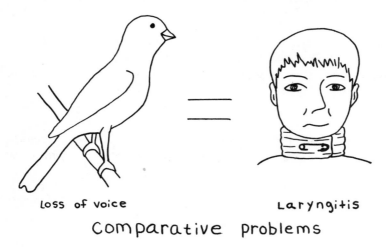

Loss of voice · · · · · · · · · · · Laryngitis

Comparative problems

HEAVY BREATHING

Respiratory sounds associated with increased or labored respiration probably reflect a *critical* condition.

Comparative problems

81

A description of other types of respiratory diseases and their complications would serve no purpose. The main thing to know is that they can happen, and if they do, consult a veterinarian immediately.

Recommendations

Besides the basics required for good health, it is most important to:

Prevent chilling to avoid respiratory problems.

Keep air clean—dust, dirt, pollutants are harmful to respiratory system and can carry disease.

Maintain humidity above 40%.

Keep nares clean.

Isolate from any other birds that might be sick or carrying disease.

Seek veterinary assistance at the first indication of any respiratory system infection.

10 FACTS and CARE: DIGESTIVE SYSTEM

The design and function of the digestive system is based upon the bird's extraordinary needs for nutrition and energy compared to other animals. The gastrointestinal tract is faced with the problem of transforming ingested food into a utilizable form of nourishment and energy for billions of cells. To visualize the size of the task, consider this example: a small bird may eat 25% of his weight in food daily. With a 20 gram canary (two-thirds of an ounce), that would be 5 grams of food. Not much volume in the palm of our hand, but compared proportionately to man, a 150 pound person would be eating 37 pounds of food. The question arises immediately of how a bird is capable of handling this volume of food, and further, how could the digestive system begin to convert this bulk to a utilizable form fast enough to provide for the energy demands?

Refinement of the digestive system specifically for the purpose of processing proportionately large volumes of food is seen in the production line design of the gastrointestinal tract. The bird has two stomachs. The first one adds digestive juices to the food as it passes through on its way to the second stomach, which rapidly grinds the food into fine particles and sends it on to the small intestine.

By having a crop as the reservoir for food, it can deliver small amounts of ingesta continually to the stomach, where it can be rapidly processed. This makes for efficiency, as it enables a relatively constant process of digestion to take place. If the bird had teeth to perform these grinding

processes instead of the gizzard, the bird would spend a long time chewing its food, which would expose it to dangers that are avoided by its bolting the food down and flying to safety. Also, it is much more efficient to have the gizzard grind food for hours in a continuous action, as the quantity of food in proportion to the size of the animal is relatively great.

As food leaves the gizzard and passes into the intestines, it is mixed with digestive juices from the liver, pancreas, and the wall of the intestine. Bile from the liver acts to neutralize the acid from the stomach and to emulsify fats in preparation for further digestion. The pancreatic juices digest proteins, fats and carbohydrates. Once the food is digested, it is absorbed by the lining of the intestine, passed on into the blood stream, and distributed through the body.

The whole process must be synchronized and efficient, as the muscular activity of the intestinal tract propels the food through the intestine rapidly. A starling will have food pass through its digestive tract in twenty minutes, and in a parakeet, it takes less than two hours. The relatively small amount of feces in the droppings indicates the thoroughness of the whole digestive process.

The digestive system is functioning under this intensity because the bird has extraordinary demands for energy. Food, the fuel for the body, is burned at a much higher rate than for any other living thing. That this is true can easily be checked by noticing that the body temperature of birds ranges anywhere from 104° to 109°.

Because energy is used rapidly, a bird must constantly depend upon food as a source of fuel. Fat reserves cannot be converted rapidly enough to energy to be of any importance. Any disturbance of the gastrointestinal tract which interferes with food digestion or absorption can cause the bird to starve to death in a few days.

The alimentary canal has many adaptions and unusual features compared to mammals. One of these, the cloaca, evolved to eliminate the need for a urinary bladder and colon. An exchange of an organ to replace two is good efficiency. To lighten the load—as needed in flight—the cloaca only collects a small volume and then empties, thus accounting for the many droppings which a bird has.

Since the cloaca has an influence on the arrangement and size of the droppings, knowing its structure makes interpretation of droppings easier. The feces enter from the large intestine on the bottom; the urine enters from the ureters (tubes leading from the kidney) at the top. When the droppings are passed, the feces fall first, with the urine (white urates and fluid urine) coming second. In many cases, this allows the urine to cover the feces. A fold from the top of the cloaca separates the terminal part of the large intestine from the area where the urine is deposited. With this arrangement, at times urine is passed as a dropping without fecal material.

The ovaduct (passage for eggs) enters the cloaca in the region of the ureters. When the female bird enters her reproductive cycle, the cloaca must enlarge to accept and pass the egg. The enlarged cloaca allows more material to collect, and thus, at this time the droppings become several times their regular size.

The capacity of the cloaca may vary from one bird to another of the same species. A 30 gram Budgerigar may have 40–70 droppings daily, depending upon the cloaca size.

Passing the Droppings

For purposes of insulation and warmth, feathers grow to the edge of the vent (opening for the passage of waste material). Thus, in the act of defecation, the feathers must be effectively parted. The bird raises his tail and combined with the increased tension of the abdominal muscles, the feathers divide. The action of the muscles of the cloaca, combined with the flicking of the tail, causes a temporary eversion and prevents any part of the elimination from adhering to the vent. This action is very rapid and the tail drops immediately.

Any time feathers are missing from around the vent or if the feathers in this area are soiled with feces, it can be concluded that the bird currently has or has had diarrhea.

INTERPRETATION OF DROPPINGS

The bird owner has many good reasons to watch droppings daily. In fact, they are one of the best indices of the bird's health.

Since birds effectively hide their sicknesses from our view, every means is taken to recognize signs of sickness in pet birds. Because the droppings provide us with a wealth of information about the bird's health, it behooves us to watch them daily. A bird that develops diarrhea doesn't cause any mess in the house, nor is the diarrhea odoriforous. It is easy for the diarrhea to go unnoticed. If the dog had a similar diarrhea in the house, there is no doubt he would be taken to the veterinarian to have his problem corrected immediately. Likewise, if the dog started urinating in the house or started to wet the area where he slept at night, the owners would be disturbed and would have immediate veterinary care. The bird which is urinating more frequently than usual is fortunate to have his master even notice it. Urinary and intestinal problems could go on for weeks or months without the owner suspecting that something is wrong. Possibly the dog owner who takes his pet to the veterinarian for diarrhea may be more concerned about the mess in the house than the animal's health. With the bird, we don't even have a situtation that irritates the household.

The bird depends upon a concerned owner and is much more dependent upon a giving master than the dog or cat is.

With reasonable awareness, information can be gleaned about the following:

VOLUME OF FOOD INGESTED

Because the bird's digestive system is short and efficient, the food which he eats today is passed through the intestinal tract today. Therefore, the fecal portion of the droppings reflects the quantity of food that he has eaten that specific day. The bird which fills his crop in the morning will pass feces all day even though eating no more until evening. The overnight droppings relate to the evening feeding.

A sick bird that consumes only half his regular volume of food will immediately reflect it as a decrease of half the normal volume. This same sick bird might be drinking an increased amount of water and thus passing more urine (white urates and watery urine). Thus, there could be just as many droppings, but of urine content not fecal material.

FUNCTIONING OF THE DIGESTIVE SYSTEM

The normal fecal elimination from the bowel has a green to black color, a finely granular texture, and carries the shape of the intestinal tract. Many factors have an influence on this description. Departure from the standard norm occurs primarily with the type of food in the diet.

Even when functioning normally, the feces will be eliminated in different colors, depending upon the rate of passage through the intestinal tract, the type of food ingested, and the amount of water it contains. Bulky food, such as greens, passes through more rapidly and makes a green, soft stool. More concentrated foods make a drier, darker stool.

Problems of abnormal function may include:

Whole seed being passed in the droppings

87

The droppings becoming a light color
The feces changing to a coarser texture
Large bulky droppings from incomplete digestion

Other problems of abnormal function would require laboratory tests for their detection.

In general, when the digestive system is not functioning properly, food is not being digested. The effect is the same as if the bird were not eating sufficient amounts of food. This, in effect, would cause an increased hunger and a weight loss. Some of these birds may be eating twice as much as usual and still be losing weight.

ABNORMALITIES OF THE INTESTINAL TRACT

Before attempting to evaluate droppings for abnormalities, a person should know normals. As a variation in size and consistency occurs between healthy birds, a normal should be established for each individual. This would best be done at the time the bird is purchased, as it will also serve to confirm the bird's health at that time. The stool has a range of shapes and colors according to the food ingested. In the course of 24 hours, some stools will be passed that appear unnatural, but the majority conform to the standard. This type of happening occurs and should not cause alarm. If the majority of the droppings lack their normal shape, an intestinal tract problem exists. The presence of irregular droppings warns of a problem but does not tell the cause of the problem. The following list of items should be considered:

INFECTIONS—Virus Bacteria Yeast Fungus

PARASITES

DIET—Moldy Foods, Decomposed Foods, Toxic Foods, Foods Irritating to the Intestinal Tract

PROBLEMS THAT AFFECT OTHER PARTS OF THE BODY—May secondarily cause diarrhea: Hepatitis, Nephritis, Pancreatitis

The following irregularities may be seen in the droppings of birds with intestinal tract problems:

RED BLOOD—Recent bleeding in the lower bowel.

BLACK BLOOD—Digested blood from the upper intestinal tract.

BROWN WATERY FECES—Severe infection—patient is critical.

MUCOUS COATING THE STOOL OR IN A LUMP ATTACHED TO THE END OF THE DROPPING—Indicates a chronic problem which may have existed for some time.

DARK GREEN BILE—The bird is not eating and is only passing bile. This patient is critical and needs immediate intensive care.

SOFT STOOLS WITH NO SHAPE—Diarrhea condition which needs diagnosis and proper treatment.

NO STOOLS AND NO BILE—Bird may be constipated or the intestinal tract blocked from some other problem.

HALF THE STOOL WITH NO SHAPE AND THE OTHER HALF WITH FORM—Diarrhea condition which needs proper diagnosis and treatment.

FUNCTIONING OF THE URINARY SYSTEM

The kidneys serve a vital role in establishing and controlling the water balance of the body. The normal kidney, then, has the responsibility of maintaining the body at a rather static water level. In one 24-hour period, the kidneys could pass quantities of fluid urine and also pass very concentrated urine, and the assumption could be made that these are normal kidneys; if they were abnormal, they would lose their ability to fluctuate between very concentrated urine and a very dilute urine.

Urine passes from the kidneys as white crystals of uric acid and as watery urine. Most birds pass both forms of urine under normal conditions. When water is in short supply, birds have the ability of conserving their own body water, and urinate solid urine as white uric acid crystals. When a bird drinks more or eats food with a high water content, he passes more watery urine.

Depending upon a bird's eating habits, some birds have a yellow pigment in their blood that is passed through the kidneys and is recognized in the dropping as yellow urates. These yellow colored urates may give some cause for concern, as about the same color develops if a bird is becoming jaundiced. If a person notices these yellow urates and the bird is not perfectly healthy, the bird should be examined by a veterinarian to determine if the bird has hepatitis.

FUNCTIONING OF THE REPRODUCTIVE SYSTEM

The cloaca of the female bird about to lay eggs will enlarge to be able to accept the egg from the vagina. The enlarged cloaca will be noticed by the size of the droppings that are passed. The droppings can become many times their normal size, but have every other characteristic of a normal dropping.

Should red blood be noted in the droppings, care should be taken in deciding if it is related to the intestinal tract, urinary tract, the cloaca, or possibly, the female system. In many cases, a retained egg in the uterus and vagina will cause bleeding. The important point to remember is that blood in the droppings can indicate trouble in other areas than the intestine and a proper diagnosis is hurriedly needed.

THOSE PROBLEMS WHICH DISTURB WATER BALANCE (general infections, liver and pancreatitive diseases)

Disease conditions often cause an increased water loss by the body. This change from normal can be detected in the droppings as increased urination; the droppings will be wetter. To replace these fluids, the bird will increase its water consumption. In these cases, the wetter droppings are only an added clue that the bird has a medical problem. Generally, there will be other signs that the bird is sick: singing or talking less, decreased activity, feathers ruffled, and sleeping more.

There are problems which occur in the hormone system that cause the bird to urinate large quantities of water. The conditions are extreme, calling for immediate diagnosis and treatment.

"Rule of Thumb" to General Health

CONDITION	% DECREASE IN VOLUME OF DROPPINGS IN 24 HOURS	BUDGERIGAR— NUMBER OF DROPPINGS IN 24 HOURS
NORMAL	NORMAL VOLUME	40–60
MODERATELY SICK	10–25%	30–40
SERIOUSLY	25–50%	20–30
CRITICAL	50% or more	Less than 20

In these instances only the fecal portion of the droppings volume is estimated or counted.

Normal droppings of Budgerigar

11 33 DANGERS

In the course of everyday living sometimes we fail to notice the dangerous situations close at hand. Following are a list of potential dangers to your bird:

TRANSPARENT WINDOW GLASS

When a bird is allowed to free fly in your home, it will not recognize window glass and very likely will attempt to fly through it. Birds have been badly hurt and killed from such accidents. Initially, keep your curtains and draperies closed and then part them gradually as it becomes more familiar with the room.

OPEN WINDOWS AND DOORS (WITHOUT A SCREEN)

In the summertime any number of birds escape from homes because of open windows and doors.

MIRRORS

Mirrors have the same intrinsic dangers as transparent glass. Once your bird has become accustomed to mirrors in the room he will enjoy them as the bird on the other side will fascinate him.

CATS AND DOGS

Most cats will believe that small birds are fair game and will seek every opportunity to eat your canary, parakeet or finch. For the people who own or want a cat, the best suggestion is to obtain the cockatiel or larger parrot. An extremely vicious cat might attack these birds, but the average house cat won't touch them.

Over a period of time a dog can be trained not to bother a free flying bird. It pays to be precautious, and the bird should be introduced to the dog gradually.

PEOPLE

The informed bird owner who takes the care of his bird judiciously and seeks consultation early is truly the bird's best friend. More birds die from uninformed owners than probably any other reason.

OPEN BOWLS AND PANS OF WATER

Something seems to attract birds to water—possibly because it shines and glitters. Birds have been known to fly into pans of boiling water, into bathtubs, toilet bowls, indoor swimming pools, etc. If your bird scalds himself, call your veterinarian immediately. Should he just get wet in a bowl of water, pat and dry him with a towel and keep him in a warm area until he is dry.

Pet birds do not swim and thus will drown if their feet cannot touch bottom.

LOUD NOISES

Birds enjoy many types of sounds and will be heard to sing and chatter along with them. Noises which begin to bother the human ear could also bother the bird. One parrot picked his feathers out whenever the people in this particular house shouted at each other.

FANS

The danger of an open fan speaks for itself.

INACTIVITY

Beware of subtle signs of sickness. The birds hide their problems amazingly well and can be seriously sick showing only a decreased activity. These birds need prompt veterinary service.

NESTING MATERIALS MADE OF THREAD

Any cloth or material which will fray with threadlike ends serves as a real danger to the feet and legs of birds. The loose thread wraps around the toes and feet of a bird acting as a tourniquet. The thread will cut through the tissues with the potential loss of toes or feet.

MANGE

Mange can be one of the causes of an abnormally shaped beak or lesions on the toes and feet. These problems should be looked into by a veterinarian.

LEG BANDS

Breeders need identification on their baby birds. Aluminum bands are slipped over the toes onto the leg when the birds are only a few days old.

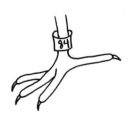

After the birds are sold, the leg band no longer has any purpose and should be removed. The two chief dangers of leg bands on a bird are one, the band will catch on some object in the cage and cause the bird to fracture its leg, two, scales will build up under the leg band causing it to act as a tourniquet on the leg. The area will swell which almost seems to incorporate the band into the leg. Recognizing the problem in this stage is almost too late. If the band stays on, the bird will lose it's foot; if the band is removed, there is risk that the leg can be broken or that the blood vessels will be damaged and result in nicrosis (dry gangrene).

OVERHEATING

Most animals can tolerate cold much better than heat, and the bird is no exception. A bird left in the sunshine on a hot day with no chance to seek shelter will die from being overheated. Birds enjoy heat and they enjoy the sunshine, when it becomes excessive the bird's system cannot tolerate it. Sick birds can be placed in incubators which may range anywhere from 85 to about 95° depending upon the seriousness of the problem and tolerate the heat very well. As these birds return to normal, the incubators become too warm for them and they draw their feathers very close to their bodies, holding their wings away from their bodies which helps eliminate the dead air space. At this point they will also be panting. When conditions such as these are noticed on birds, it is time to get them to a cooler area.

CARBON MONOXIDE, PAINT FUMES AND SMOKE

Any contaminant in the air is potentially harmful to a bird. Schoolteachers enjoy informing their classes that in the olden days, miners took birds into the mine shafts with them as a safety measure. The birds are quickly affected by poisonous gases. Their critical appearance would be a warning for the miners. The same can be true in private homes. There was an instance where a woman became hysterical because of the death one afternoon of her five birds. She telephoned the veterinarian frantically and was immediately warned to leave the house as poisonous gases were in the atmosphere. In fact, there had been a defect in their furnace which had allowed carbon monoxide to work its way into the forced air system in sufficient quantity to kill the birds and not yet affect the owner. Had the birds not died and she had stayed in the house, she too would have succumbed to the poisonous gas.

BURNT TEFLON

Teflon-coated pans bear no warning that poisonous gases are expelled if burnt. A burnt teflon pan causes no danger to the people in the home or in the room where this has happened, but birds will die from exposure to these fumes.

POISONOUS PLANTS

A number of common house plants and garden ornamentals are toxic to birds if ingested. Ivy, poinsettia, and a species of dieffenbachia are included in a list of potentially dangerous plants listed in Current Veterinary Therapy.

INSECTICIDES

Almost all insecticides are potentially poisonous to birds. Aerosols sprayed into the room to kill insects can kill your bird.

PEST STRIPS—Are in the same class as insecticides.

MEDICINES

A person hardly realizes how many toxic materials are around until he starts handling birds. Medicines which seemingly are safe for people can kill birds. Be extremely careful in the administration of any drug; a bird is so tiny that overdoses of drugs are very easy—and overdoses can kill. As with yourself, handle medicines reverently.

Antibiotics and other drugs sold in the pet shop for your bird should only be used when veterinary help is not available. Adding medicine to the drinking water can result in underdosages which will of course do your bird no good or may result in over dosages which might be toxic to your bird. Drug dosages must be calculated for the exact weight of the bird. This is the only safe way to use medicine. If your bird is seriously ill and no veterinary attention is available, treat your bird with the medicine at hand.

There are poor bird products on the market with deceiving names.

WOOD CHIPS

Wood chips are sometimes used in the pans of large birds to absorb the droppings and as the method of keeping the cage clean. Particularly, young birds may get into these wood chips and eat them as food. Some very valuable baby macaws and cockatiels have died as a result of impaction following the eating of wood chips.

VITAMIN B DEFICIENCY

Vitamin B Complex is mainly found in the hull of the seed. If you have watched pet birds eat, they remove the hull from the seed thus leaving the part containing most of the vitamin B complex fall to the bottom of the cage. No wonder than that this is a commonly seen deficiency. Read the label on the vitamin product you are putting in the bird's drinking water to be sure that it contains the vitamin B complex vitamins.

SMALL CAGES

One feels sorry for birds confined to a small cage.

TOYS

As with children, toys can be dangerous. Any sharp projection, wire, hook, or fiber could catch on the bird's feet or legs. Stay away from junk toys, and inspect closely anything you put in the bird's cage.

LONG TOENAILS

If birds could talk, overgrown nails would be one of the most common complaints.

OVERGROWN BEAKS

Overgrown beaks can create a serious problem for the bird as it inhibits normal eating.

OIL OR GREASE ON FEATHERS

Since the chief purpose of feathers is to keep the bird warm, anything that would damage or destroy the insulating powers of feathers would be deleterious to the bird. Any oil or grease on the downy feathers will mat these feathers so that they cannot insulate the bird's body. Avoid using Vaseline, a commonly used preparation for areas of inflammation or irritation on people. It is probably in the medicine chest of every home in the United States.

The bird owner observes what appears to be an itching problem, concludes that there must be a problem with the skin in that area and applies vaseline to help the bird's problem. The oil which had been applied to the skin is not satisfied to remain in one area and much like putting oil on the corner of a blotter gradually spreads to other areas infecting the insulating area over a large portion of the bird's body. The bird will react to the insult by trying to remove the grease as best he can. He will seem to be picking and itching more but actually will be fighting for his survival. If the problem is minimal, the bird may overcome it. If there is sufficient grease on the skin and feathers, the bird will chill and die in a period of time.

Even small amounts of vaseline applied to the toes or legs can be troublesome as the bird does help clean himself with his feet and thus rubs the oil from his legs onto the feathers of his body. Whenever a bird's feathers look wet or pasted together from oil, it is a warning that there is a severe problem.

The *cardinal* rule is do not apply any oil or oily substance to the skin or feathers of a bird.

CAGED DOOR UNSECURE

Watch those cage doors! It is not unusual that birds escape from their cages through doors that are either left ajar or whose locking mechanism has become worn. The doors on about half of the cages (especially those of the bigger birds) are defective and need additional support to their locking mechanism.

PLACING BIRDS TOGETHER IN A COMMON CAGE

Mixing birds can be dangerous for several reasons. They don't always get along together and can bite and pick viciously until the death of one of them. Also, one bird may dominate the other one until finally the bird is mentally affected by it, deteriorates and finally dies. Third, one bird may reign over the seed cups and deny the other bird's access to them, in which case the bird would gradually starve to death.

LEAD—IN PAINT, COLORED PICTURES, LABELS

These products may contain sufficient lead pigment to be toxic. Death from all these sources happens too frequently. Be careful.

AIR POLLUTION

Whenever the news media broadcasts an ozone warning, include your bird as one of those animals which might be affected. Although not lethal, you might notice that your bird becomes inactive and seems stressed.

HOT AIR DUCT

Direct heat blowing on a bird from a hot forced air furnace can be fatal in a matter of hours.

CAGE DECORATIONS

Ribbons or any type fabric decorations used to decorate the cage (as at Christmas) are subject to being chewed and shredded. The threads entangle the bird or his limbs and can either trap him or act as tourniquets.

VAL CLAMPS

Home made cages for large psittacine birds sometimes use val clamps to attach the doors. Parrots remove these and get them caught on their beaks. Avoid fracture to the jaw when taking the clamps off. The mandible is not solid bone and can be broken.

BOTULISM

Particularly a danger for outside birds, any bird eating rotten food or other decomposed organic material will die from this toxin.

CARPET

A bird picking or tearing fibers off pieces of carpeting and swallowing them can impact their crops.

For other dangers see section on Food Dangers.

12 SIGNS OF SICKNESS & EMERGENCY TREATMENT

Signs of Sickness

Birds hide their problems very effectively, and when they begin to obviously manifest their illness, they are already seriously to critically ill. The bird that dies "suddenly'" has probably been sick for some time and was just not recognized as being abnormal. Birds are actually very hardy and tolerate problems as well as any animal. If given a chance, birds live long.

Because of this difficulty in detecting illness early, the following is recommended:

Observe *closely* for any sign of illness.

TAKE YOUR BIRD TO THE VETERINARIAN ANNUALLY FOR A CHECKUP. This will include a physical examination, a 24-hour dropping analysis and a blood test (total protein and pack cell volume).

Critically sick bird.

Watch for any of these signs of sickness:

Change in the character of the droppings or a decrease in the
number or volume.

Change in food or water consumption.

Change in attitude—generally observed as decreased activity (inac-
tivity) or talking less, singing less, or no response to stimuli.

Change in bird's appearance or posture. A sick bird generally ruffles
his feathers, begins closing his eyes in a sleepy fashion, and will be
sitting low on the perch (droopy).

Any noticeable breathing while resting, heavy breathing after exer-
tion, change in character of voice, and any respiratory sounds—
sneeze, wheeze or click.

Any enlargement—even fat is abnormal in a bird.

comparative problems

*A bird with ruffled feathers and partially closed
eyes—A sick person requiring intensive care.*

comparative problems

A bird lying on the bottom of a cage is probably dying.

Emergency Treatment

(Temporary Care Until the Bird Can be Seen by a Veterinarian)

If ever the bird sits with its feathers ruffled, eyes partially closed, droopy appearance, or if there are signs of diarrhea or respiratory problems, the bird should be treated immediately. Also, any bird which has been injured, sustained a broken leg or wing, bitten by a cat, dog or other animal, burned or chilled, should likewise be started on emergency care.

Every part of the following treatment is *important!*

INCUBATOR

A temporary incubator can be made by placing a heating pad along side the cage and then the entire cage is wrapped with plastic and a cage cover. An infrared light or 150 watt light bulb could be used as an alternate heat source. The temperature should be maintained at 80–85°.

Should the cage temperature become too hot, the bird will start breathing rapidly, hold his wings out from the sides of his body, and the feathers will be held so close or tight to the body that he will appear peculiarly skinny.

FOOD

A bird that stops eating dies. Therefore, every effort must be made to encourage the bird to eat. Cups of food should be placed adjacent to where the bird is perched, food scattered on the bottom of the cage if the bird is off his perch. The veterinarian will immediately force feed a bird by passing a stomach tube.

REST

Sick birds need rest, and thus, should be in a darkened room or covered to insure 12 to 16 hours of sleep. A two-hour nap in the morning or afternoon is advisable.

DROPPINGS

Start counting droppings. The number or volume of droppings will be of great concern to the veterinarian. Better yet, save the droppings for the veterinarian to view.

DON'TS

    a. Don't give whiskey.
    b. Don't use laxatives.
    c. Don't use oil.
    d. Don't stop food.

TELEPHONE YOUR VETERINARIAN

INDEX